AF434651

Is Grave-Worship Bidah or Shirk? You Decide

Dr. Muddassir Khan

Bismillahir Rahmaanir Raheem.

In the Name of Allah, The Most Merciful, The Bestower of Mercy.

INTRODUCTION

All praise to Allaah. We praise Him, seek His help, and ask for His forgiveness. And we repent to Him and seek refuge in Him from the evil of ourselves and our deeds. Whoever Allaah guides, no one can lead him astray, and whoever gets lost, no one can guide him. I testify that there is no divinity worthy of worship except Allaah, and I testify that Muhammad is His slave and messenger, may the peace and blessings of Allaah be upon him, his family, his companions, and those who followed them in righteousness until the Day of Judgment.

Allah has informed us in the Quran first and foremost that He did not create the *jinn* or humans, except to worship Allah. The Ulamah (Scholars) of Tafseer have explained that this verse includes many aspects of Ibaadah (worship). The first thing we should do is to know Allah. If we don't know our Rabb (Lord); if we don't know what Allah has ordained upon us, then how can we fulfill the obligation of Ibadah (worship)?

Every Ibaadah (worship) that is compulsory upon a

Muslim (Fard) learning the rulings of how to fulfill it correctly is also Fard (compulsory).

Is prayer fard on you? Yes. Then learning the fiqh (how to do it) of Salah (prayer) is also fard on you. Is Siyaam (fasting) in Ramadan fard on you? Yes. Then learning the fiqh of how to correctly fast is fard on you (compulsory). It's an obligation. Individually everyone has to learn this knowledge. This is an individual obligation on every Muslim.

A Muslim should also know what all constitutes Ibaadah. All Muslims agree that Grave Worship is not Islamic.

But is it a Bidah (Worshipping Allaah in ways that are not those of the Prophet, peace and blessings of Allaah be upon him, or his rightly guided successors)? When a person does Bidah he is worshipping Allah alone but in a new way which was not taught by Allah and His Messenger (peace and blessings of Allah be upon him).

Or it Shirk (associating partners with Allah)? With Shirk a person does not worship Allah alone but worships and asks for help from someone besides Allah.

This book gives you evidence from the Quran, Sunnah, and Scholarly Statements regarding Grave Worship and whether it is Bidah or Shirk.

Quran and Sunnah

Allah, the Exalted, has said in his Book which he has revealed for the guidance of mankind (the Quran) which is a healing and mercy for the believers:

"You (Alone) we worship and You (Alone) we seek help from (for each and everything)."

(*Surah al-Fatiha*: 5)

An-Nu'maan ibn Basheer (Allah be pleased with him) narrated that the Messenger of Allah (peace and blessings of Allah be upon him) said: "Du'aa' (supplication or asking for help) is worship."

Allah, the Exalted, said, disapproving the beliefs of the polytheists and their actions, and also to reprimand them:

"Say: Call upon other (gods) whom you assert (to be associate gods) besides Allah: They have no power not

*the weight of an atom (or a small ant) — in the heavens
or on earth: No (sort of) share have they therein, nor is
any of them a Helper to Allah."*

(*Surah Saba' 22*)

Allah, the Glorified and Exalted, said:

*"Such is Allah your Lord: to Him belongs all Dominion.
And those whom you invoke besides Him have not the
least power. If you invoke them, they will not listen to
your call, and if they were to listen, they cannot answer
your (prayer). On the Day of Judgement, they will reject
your partnership. And none (O man) can inform you
(the truth), like the one who is acquainted with all
things (the All-Knower)."*

(*Surah Fatir 14*)

Explaining their mischief and unfolding their blemish
Allah said:

*"Say: Have you seen (these) partners of yours whom you
call upon besides Allah? Show me what it is they have*

created in the (wide) earth. Or have they a share in the heavens? Or have we given them a Book from which they (can derive) clear (evidence)? No, rather the wrong-doers promise each other nothing but delusions."

(*Surah Faatir 40*)

Emphasizing, Allah said to them:

"But those you call upon besides Him (Allah), are unable to help you, and indeed to help themselves."

(*Surah al-A'raf 197*)

Allah also says:

"Nor have you, besides Allah, anyone to protect or to help."

(*Surah al-Shura 31*)

Allah ordered His Prophet (peace and blessings of Allah be upon him) to ask the polytheists and the seekers of help from others besides Allah to reply to His question:

"Say: See you then? The things that you invoke besides Allah — can they, if Allah wills some harm for me, remove His harm? Or if he wills some mercy for me. can they keep back His Mercy?"

(*Surah al-Zumar 38*)

"Or, who listens to the distressed (soul) when it calls on Him, and who relieves its suffering, and makes you (mankind) inheritors of the earth? Can there be another god besides Allah? Little it is that you remember."

(*Surah al-Naml 27:62*)

He then intended to make them understand saying:

"Verily those whom you call upon besides Allah are servants like you. So call upon them and let them answer you, if you are indeed truthful."

(*Surah al-A'raf 194*)

He also said:

"Say: Do you then take (for worship) protectors other than Him, such as have no power either for good or for harm to themselves."

(*Surah Ra'd 16*)

He (Allah) then rebuked them saying:

"(The pagans and those who worship other than Allah), invoke nothing besides Him, but call upon female deities. They call but upon Satan, the persistent rebel!"

(*Surah al-Nisa 117*)

He then gave a decision saying:

"And who is more astray than one who invokes besides Allah, such as will not answer him till the day of judgment, and who (in fact) are unaware of their call (to them)."

(*Surah al-Ahqaf 5*)

Allah, the Exalted, has mentioned in the Quran many prophets and His pious servants. They were in need of seeking assistance and help from Him and prayed to Him to help them in their problems and calamities that befell them. They never sought help from anyone, nor did they call anyone but upon their Lord alone. From Adam to Nuh, from Ibrahim to Musa, from Yunus to the last Prophet, Muhammad b. Abdallah (peace be upon all of them), all asked only from Allah. Some asked Allah for forgiveness, or a child, or healing, or deliverance from problems, trials, or ruin on account of an injury, poverty, and imprisonment. They did not ask anyone but Allah alone.

If any calamity befell a servant of Allah he always sought help from Him alone.

The Prophet (peace and blessings of Allah be upon him) said to his cousin Abdallah b. Abbas (Allah be pleased with him): "If you ask for anything, ask Allah for it; if you seek help, seek it from Allah; whatever you will meet in your future life, that has been decreed for you; if all the creatures strive to benefit you, they cannot benefit you but to the extent, Allah has decreed for you; if they strive to harm you, they cannot harm you but to the extent, Allah has decreed against you."

The following words of Allah, the Exalted, apply to them:

"When it is said to them: Follow what Allah has revealed: They say: Nay, we shall follow the ways of our fathers. What! even though their fathers did not understand anything nor were they guided."

(Surah al-Baqarah 170)

Allah said:

"When my servants ask them concerning Me, I am indeed close (to them): I listen to the prayer of every supplicant when he calls on Me: Let them also, with a will, listen to My call, and believe in Me: that they may walk in the right way."

(Surah al-Baqarah 186)

(*Surah Ghafir 60*)

The Messenger of Allah (peace and blessings of Allah be upon him) came to take unbelievers of Mecca, the polytheists of Arabia, and the idolators of the pre-Islamic days, out from misguidance and polytheism, and to purify them from idol-worship and polytheism. Similarly, did the Messengers of Allah who come before him.

Allah says:

"*There is none who has the right to be worshipped but He (Allah). It is He who gives life and causes death*"

(*Surah al-Dukhan 8*)

"*Blessed be He in Whose Hand is the dominion and He over all things has Power.*"

(*Surah al-Mulk 1*)

*"Say: In Whose Hand is the governance of all things,
Who protects (all) but against Whom there is no
protector...?"*

(Surah al-Mu'minun 88)

*"So glory to Him in whose hands is the dominion of all
things: and to Him will you all be brought back."*

(Surah Ya-Sin 36:83)

*"For Allah is He who gives (all) sustenance, — Lord of
Power, the Most Strong."*

(Surah al-Dhariyat 58)

*"There is no moving creature on earth but its sustenance
is due from Allah."*

(Surah Hud 6)

*"How many are the creatures that carry not their own
sustenance: It is Allah who feeds (both) them and you:*

for He hears and knows all things.”

(Surah al-Ankabut 60)

“Say: verily my Lord enlarges and restricts the provision to whom He pleases.”

(Surah Saba’ 39)

“Say: O Allah, Lord of power (and rule), You give power to whom you please, and You strip off power from whom You please: You endow with honor whom You please, and You bring low whom You please; in your hand is all good. Verily, over all things You have power.”

(Surah Ali Imran 26)

“The blind and the seeing are not alike; nor are the depths of darkness and the light, nor are the (chilly) shade and the (genial) heat of the sun: nor are alike those that are living and those that are dead. Allah can make any that He wills to hear; but you cannot make those to hear who are (buried) in graves.”

(*Surah Fatir 19*)

Allah, the Exalted, has said:

"Mankind was one single nation and Allah sent Messengers with glad tidings and warnings; and with them, He sent the Book in truth to judge between people in matters wherein they differed; but the people of the book, after the clear signs came to them did not differ among themselves, except through selfish stubborn resistance. Then Allah by His Grace guided the believers to the truth concerning that wherein they differed. For Allah guides whom He will to a path that is straight."

(*Surah al-Baqarah 213*)

"Say: Shall we tell you of those who lost most in respect of their deeds? They are whose efforts have been wasted in this life, while they thought that they were acquiring good by their works!"

(*Surah al-Kahf 103-104*)

He previously said about them:

"(Unbelievers) whose eyes had been under a veil from remembrance of Me, and who had been unable even to hear. Do the unbelievers think that they can take My servants as protectors besides Me? Verily, We have prepared Hell for the unbelievers for (their) entertainment."

(Surah al-Kahf 101-102)

Tafsir of a verse from the Quran

"Say (O Muhammad), I have no power over any harm or profit to myself except as Allah may will."

(Surah Yunus 49)

Nawwab Siddiq Hasan Khan, in his explanation of the Qur'an, said regarding the above verse:

This is the greatest restraint and deepest deterrent for one who has become habituated to call upon the Messenger of Allah (peace and blessings of Allah be upon him) or to seek help from him in the event of the occurrence of calamities that cannot be repelled by anyone except by Allah (Glory be to Him). Similarly, it is a deterrent for one who seeks from the Prophet that which cannot be given except by Allah. This is the position of the Lord of the Universe, who created the prophets, the pious men, and all the creatures, and who sustained them, gave them life, and will give them death. How does he ask as a prophet from the prophets, or angels from the angels, or a pious man from the pious men, for a thing over which they have no power, and which they cannot give themselves? How does he forsake seeking these things from the Lord of the Lords, the All-Powerful over everything, the Creator, the Sustainer, the Bestower, and the Restrainer? There is sufficient counsel for you in this verse, for the chief of the children of Adam, and the Last Prophet has been commanded by Allah to tell His servants: "I have no power over any harm or profit to myself," how can he then have power over it for others? How can a person other than him (the Prophet) whose rank is lower than his, and which is not equal to his rank, have the power over harm and profit to himself, let alone his power over it for others?

Curiously enough, these people (the grave-worshippers)

have clung to the tombs of the dead, who are buried under the layers of the earth. They ask them for their need over which only Allah, the Exalted, has power. Why are they not aware of their falling into polytheism, and why are they not aware of the fact that they are involved in breaking the meaning of the creed of Islam "There is no god but Allah," and the import of the Qur'anic verse: "Say: He is Allah the one and only?"

And more curious than this is the fact that the scholars are aware of the deeds these people are doing, still, they do not raise any objection to them, and they do not intervene for their return to the pagan days before Islam, rather to the belief more severe than those of the pre-Islamic Arabia. They admit that Allah, Glory be to Him, alone is the Creator, the sustainer, the Giver of life, the Giver of death, the Harmer, the Benefiter. They make their idols intercessors for them with Allah, drawing them near to Him, regard them as powerful over harm and benefit, and invoke them sometimes independently and sometimes along with Allah, the Almighty. It is sufficient for you to hear such evil. Allah is the helper of His religion, the purifier of His Sharia from the dirt of polytheism, and the filth of unbelief. The devil, may

Allah disgrace him, made it a means for his pleasure, and coolness of his heart, and he is pleased by the unbelief of a large number of these blessed people, while they think that they are acquiring good by their works. To Allah we belong and to Him is our return!

In his "Fatawa", Ibn Taymiyya relates that Bayazid al-Bistami has said: "Seeking help by the creature from another creature is like seeking help by a drowning person from another drowning person."

He further reports al-Shaikh Abu 'Abdallah al-Quraishi as saying: Seeking help by the creature from the creature is like seeking help by a prisoner from a prisoner. Moses (peace and blessings of Allah be upon him)is reported to have supplicated Allah as follows: O Allah, praise be to You, complaint is to be lodged with You, help is to be sought from You, aid is to be asked for from You, reliance is to be placed on You, and there is no might and no power except in You."

Allah says,

"And who is more astray than one who invokes besides Allah, such as will not answer him till the day of judgment, and who (In fact) are unconscious of their call (to them)?"

(Surah al-Ahqaf 5)

Allah, the Exalted, said:

"Do they indeed ascribe to Him as partners things that can create nothing, but are themselves created? No aid can they give them, nor can they aid themselves. If you call them to guidance, they will not obey: for you, it is the same whether you call them or you hold your peace. Verily those whom you call upon besides Allah are servants like unto you: call upon them, and let them listen to your prayer if you are indeed truthful. Have they feet to walk with? or eyes to see with? or ears to hear with? Say, call your god-partners, scheme (your worst) against me, and give me no respect. For my protector is Allah who revealed the Book (from time to time) and He will choose and befriend the righteous. Not

those you call upon besides Him, are unable to help you, and indeed to help themselves. If you call them for guidance, they hear not. You will see them looking at you but they see not."

(Surah al-Araf 191-198)

Allah, the Exalted, has given in the Qur'an an account of the polytheists of the Quraish of Arabia and their belief in seeking help from Allah, and asking others for aid besides Allah in the following verse:

"He It is who enables you to traverse through land and sea; so that you even board ships; they sail with them with a favorable wind, and they rejoice therein; then comes a stormy wind and the waves come to them from all sides, and they think they are being overwhelmed: they cry unto Allah, sincerely offering (their) duty only unto Him, saying: If You deliver us from this, we shall truly show our gratitude."

(Surah Yunus 22)

Allah, the Exalted, says in His Book:

*"Say: None in the heavens or on earth, except Allah,
knows what is hidden."*

(*Surah an-Naml 65*)

Allah said:

"Verily Allah knows (all) the hidden things of the
heavens and the earth. Verily, He has full knowledge or
all that is in (men's) heart."

(Surah Fatir 38)

Allah, the Exalted, said:

*"Verily, Allah knows the secrets of the heavens and the
earth: and Allah sees well all that you do."*

(*Surah al-Hujurat 18*)

*"To Allah do belong the unseen (secrets) of the heavens
and the earth, and to Him goes back every affair (for
decision)."*

(*Surah Hud 123*)

He commanded His Prophet to say:

"Say: The unseen is only for Allah (to know). Then wait you: I too will wait with you."

(*Surah Yunus 20*)

Allah, the Exalted, said:

"With Him are the keys of the unseen; the treasures that none knows there are on the earth and in the sea. Not a leaf falls but with His knowledge. There is not a grain in the darkness (or depths) of the earth, nor anything fresh or dry (green or withered) but is written in a Clear Record (to those who can read)."

(*Surah al-An'am 59*)

Allah says:

"Verily, the knowledge of the Hour is with Allah (alone).

It is He who sends down rain, and He who knows what is in the wombs. Nor does anyone know what it is that he will earn on the morrow: Nor does anyone know in what land he is to die. Verily, with Allah is full knowledge and He: is acquainted (with all things)."

(*Surah Luqman 34*)

Allah says:

"Allah knows what every female (womb) bears, by how much the wombs fall short (of their time or number) or do exceed. Every single thing is before His sight, in (due) proportion. He knows the unseen and that which is open: He is the great, the Most High."

(*Surah Ra'd 8-9*)

Allah says:

"Verily, the hour is coming, and My Will is to keep it hidden, for every soul to receive its reward by the measure of its endeavor."

(*Surah TaHa 15*)

Addressing Himself to His Prophet Allah, the Exalted, said:

"They ask you about the (final) Hour when will be Its appointed time? Say: 'The knowledge thereof is with my Lord (alone): None but He can reveal as to when it will occur. Heavy were its burden through the heavens and the earth. Only, all of a sudden will it come to you.' They ask you as if you have a good knowledge of it. Say: 'The knowledge thereof is with Allah (alone), but most men know not.'"

(*Surah al-A'raf 187*)

Allah, the Exalted, also said:

"People ask you concerning the Hour, say: 'The knowledge thereof is with Allah (alone).'"

(*Surah al-Ahzab 63*)

Allah, the Exalted, said:

"He it is Who created you from clay, and decreed a stated term (for you). And there is in His presence another determined term (for you to be resurrected); yet you doubt within yourselves (in the Resurrection)."

(Surah al-An'am 2)

"With Him is the knowledge of the Hour (of Judgment): And to Him shall you be brought back."

(Surah al-Zukhruf 85)

"With Him are the keys of the unseen, the treasures that none knows but He."

(Surah al-An'am 59)

The Prophet (peace and blessings of Allah be upon him) himself negated the knowledge of these unseen matters and mentioned that the knowledge of the unseen is known to Allah alone.

The well-known Hadith of Jibril says that he asked the

Prophet (peace and blessings of Allah be upon him): when will the last Hour occur?

He replied: The one who is asked about it is no better informed than the one who is asking. I shall tell you about its signs. When a maid-servant begets her mistress, and the herdsman of the camels exalt themselves in buildings, (the Hour will come), as well as five things which no one but Allah knows. Then the Prophet (peace and blessings of Allah be upon him) recited: "Verily Allah has the knowledge of the Hour."

The Prophet (peace and blessings of Allah be upon him) said: "The keys of the unseen are five, and Allah alone knows them. Allah alone knows what the wombs contain; no one knows what will be on the morrow but Allah; and you do not know in what land you will die but Allah; and no one knows when the Last Hour will come but Allah."

There is also a tradition to the same effect, transmitted by Jabir (Allah be pleased with him). He said: "I heard the Prophet (peace and blessings of Allah be upon him) say one month before he died: You ask me about the

Hour. The knowledge of it is with Allah."

Allah commanded His Prophet (peace and blessings of Allah be upon him) to say:

"I have no power over any good or harm to myself except as Allah wills. If I had knowledge of the unseen, I should have multiplied all good, and no evil should have touched me: I am but a warner and a bringer of glad tidings to those who have faith."

(Surah al-A'raf 188)

"Say I tell you not that with me are the treasures of Allah, nor do I know what is hidden nor do I tell you I am an angel. I but follow what is revealed to me. Say: can the blind be held equal to the seeing? will you then consider not?"

(Surah al-An'am 50)

"One day will Allah gather the messengers together, and ask: what was the response you received (from men to your teaching)? They will say: We have no knowledge: it

is You who knows in full all that is hidden."

(*Surah al-Maidah 109*)

Similarly, Allah negated the knowledge of the unseen from His angels by saying:

"They said: Glory to you: of knowledge we have none, save what You have taught us: in truth, it is you who are perfect in knowledge and wisdom."

(*Surah al-Maidah 109*)

There are numerous such events and accounts, in the Qur'an and the Sunnah, of the Prophets from Adam to Noah, from Abraham to Moses, and from him to the last Prophet, the Chief of the Messengers (peace and blessings be upon him).

The life of the Prophet (peace and blessings of Allah be upon him) and its accounts are replete with the circumstances which decisively indicate that he (i.e. the Prophet) did not possess the knowledge of the unseen. Had he possessed it, the incidents that took place during his lifetime would not have happened, like the martyrdom of the Qur'an-readers at Bit Mu'una, Bai'at al-Ridwan, the incident of bringing the lie against A'isha, the event of the people of Uraina, and similarly many other events.

A girl said while singing: Among us, there is a Prophet who knows what will happen tomorrow. The Prophet (peace and blessings of Allah be upon him) objected to her and said: "Leave this and say what you were saying previously: No one knows what will happen tomorrow except Allah."

Allah, the Exalted, told the truth, and His Messenger (peace and blessings of Allah be upon him) told the truth, and anyone who said against it lied, as reported by Aisha Siddiqah, daughter of Abu Bakr Siddiq and wife of the Messenger of Allah (peace and blessings of Allah be upon him) with whom she had lived, and the mother of the believers (Allah be pleased with her), who said: If anyone tells you that he (i.e. the Prophet, peace and blessings of Allah be upon him) possessed the knowledge of the unseen, he tells a lie. But he says: No one knows the unseen except Allah."

Allah the Exalted, has mentioned in the Qur'an, saying:

"What kept man back from belief when Guidance came to them was nothing but this: they said: 'Has Allah sent a man (like us) to be (His) Apostle?'"

(Surah al-Isra 94)

"They (the disbelievers) said: You are no more than human, like ourselves. You wish to turn us away from the (gods) our fathers used to worship. Then bring us some clear authority."

(Surah Ibrahim 10)

The prophets admitted that they were human beings:

"Their messengers said to them: True we are human like yourselves, but Allah does grant His grace to such of His servants as He pleases."

(Surah Ibrahim 11)

Describing the events of the people of Antioch, Allah said:

"Set forth to them, by way of a parable, the (story of) the Companions of the city. Behold, there come Messengers to it. When we (first) sent to them two apostles, they rejected them: But We strengthened them with a third: They said: Truly, we have been sent on a mission to you. The (people) said: 'You are only men like ourselves.'"

(Surah Ya-Sin 14-15)

He has mentioned the account of Pharaoh and his Chiefs in the following words:

"Then we sent Moses and his brother Aaron with our signs and authority manifest to Pharaoh and his Chiefs: but these behaved insolently. They were arrogant people. They said: 'Shall we believe in two men like ourselves.'"

(Surah al-Mu'minun 45-46)

He has given a detailed description of the people of Noah when he was sent to them:

"The Chiefs of the unbelievers among his people said: He is no more than a man like ourselves: his wish is to assert his superiority over you: if Allah had wished (to send messengers), He could have sent down angels: never did we hear such a thing (as he says) among our ancestors of old. (And some said): He is only a man possessed."

(*Surah al-Mu'minun 24-25*)

He has depicted an account of Thamud, the people of Salih (peace and blessings of Allah be upon him). They uttered the same words:

"He is no more than a man like yourselves. He eats of that of which you eat, and drinks of what you drink. If you obey a man like yourselves, behold it is certain you will be lost."

(*Surah al-Mu'minun 33-34*)

The companions of the wood (Ashab al-Aika) also spoke the same words to Shu'aib:

"You are no more than a mortal (man) like us and we think that you are a liar."

(Surah al-Shu'ara' 186)

The unbelievers of Makkah also said the same words to the last Prophet (peace and blessings of Allah be upon him):

"The wrong-doers conceal their private counsels, (saying), 'Is this one more than a man like yourselves? will you go to witchcraft with your open eyes.'"

(Surah al-Anbiya 3)

Allah replies to them in the following words:

"Before you (O Muhammad), also, the apostles We sent were but men, to whom We granted inspiration: if you realize this not, ask of those who possess the message."

(Surah al-Anbiya 7)

Allah, the Exalted, commanded His Prophet (peace and blessings of Allah be upon him) to say:

"Say: I am but a man like yourselves (but) the inspiration has come to me, that your God is one God."

(Surah al-Kahf 110)

He explained to the people, in general, the nature of the great Messenger of Allah (peace and blessings of Allah be upon him) in the following words:

"Allah did confer a great favor on the believers when He sent among them an apostle from among themselves."

(Surah Al-Imran 164)

The Prophet (peace and blessings of Allah be upon him) said about himself:

"I am but a man like you: I am caused to forget, as you forget. So when I forget, remind me."

A'isha (Allah be pleased with her), the mother of the

believers, said about the Messenger of Allah (peace and blessings of Allah be upon him):

"He was but a man from mankind: he washed his clothes, milked his sheep, and served himself."

The address of Allah, the Exalted, to His Prophet (peace and blessings of Allah be upon him) after He mentioned the events of Moses (peace and blessings of Allah be upon him):

"You were not on the western side when We decreed the Commission to Moses nor were you a witness of these events."

(Surah al-Qasas 44)

He also said:

"But you were nor a dweller among the people of Madyan, rehearsing our signs to them; but it is He who sends Apostles (with inspiration)."

(Surah al-Qasas 45)

He also said:

"Nor were you at the side of (the Mountain of) Tur when we called to Moses. Yet (are you sent) as a mercy from the Lord, to give warning to a people to whom no warner had come before you: in order that they may receive admonition."

(*Surah al-Qasas 46*)

Allah said to His Prophet after relating the story of Mary (Maryam):

"You were not with them when they cast lots with arrows, as to which of them should be charged with the care of Mary: nor were you with them when they disputed the point."

(*Surah Ali-Imran 44*)

Before it He (Allah) mentioned the events of Noah and Joseph (peace be upon them) to him, as in the following verse:

"Such are some of the stories of the unseen, which We have revealed unto you: before this, neither you nor the people knew them. So persevere patiently, for the end is for those who are righteous."

(Surah Hud 49)

"Say you: This is my way: I do invite unto Allah—on evidence clear as the seeing with one's eyes — I and whoever follows me. Glory to Allah! and never will I join gods with Allah."

(Surah Yusuf 108)

The sayings of great Hanafi Scholars:

The Grave-Worshippers falsely claim their ascription to the Hanafis, but they have no connection with them. Neither the Quran supports them, nor the Sunna supports them, nor the Hanafi Fiqh.

Plastering the graves and building erection over the tombs have been forbidden by the Prophet (peace and blessings of Allah be upon him). A tradition from him says: The Messenger of Allah (peace and blessings of Allah be upon him) forbade the plastering of the grave with gypsum, sitting on it, and building erection over it."

It has been narrated from Abu'l— Hayyaj al—Asadi (Allah be pleased with him) that he said: " Ali (Allah be pleased with him) said to me: Should I not send you on the same mission as Allah's Messenger had sent me? Do not leave an image but obliterate it; and a high grave but level it (make it parallel with the ground)."

'Umar b. al-Harith narrated on the authority of Thumama that he said: " We were with Fadala b. 'Ubaid in the country of the Romans at a place (known as) Rudis, when a friend of ours died. Fadala b. 'Ubaid ordered to prepare: a grave for him and then it was leveled, and he said: I heard the Messenger of Allah (peace and blessings of Allah be upon him) commanding (us) to level the grave."

Muhammad b. al-Hasan ashShaibani has reported his teacher Abu Hanifa (Allah have mercy on them) as saying: "My teacher has narrated to me attributing it to the Prophet (peace and blessings of Allah be upon him) that he forbade constructing the graves, quadrangular and plastering them with gypsum."

Imam Muhammad b. al-Hasan,. the disciple of Abu Hanifa was asked: "Do you disapprove of the plastering of the graves with gypsum?" He said: "Yes".

Al—Sarakhsi said in his "al—Mabsut": "The graves should not be plastered with gypsum, as it has been narrated from, the Prophet (peace and blessings of Allah be upon him) that he forbade the plastering of the graves with gypsum and constructing them, quadrangular."

An eminent Hanafi judge Hasan b. al-Mansur, surnamed Qadi Khan, said in his Fatawa: "The grave should not be plastered with gypsum, nor should any erection be built over it, as Abu Hanifa is reported to have said: 'The grave should not be plastered with gypsum or with earth, and no erection be constructed over it.'"

Al—Kasani said: "The plastering of the grave with gypsum or with the earth is disapproved (makruh); Abu Hanifa disapproved of making any erection over the grave and putting any mark bn it. Abu Yusuf disapproved of writing on the grave."

Al—Karkhi has mentioned it on the basis of a tradition narrated by Jabir b. 'Abdallah from the Prophet (peace and blessings of Allah be upon him) that he said: Do not plaster the graves, nor build any erection over them, nor sit, nor write on them.

Al-Kasani then continues: For this belongs to decoration, and the dead does not need it. Further, it is a wastage of property. Hence it is disapproved (makruh).

Moreover, it is also disapproved that the earth is taken out from the grave to be increased, for it is excess to it like making an erection. There is no harm in sprinkling water over the grave, for this is meant for leveling it. Abu Yusuf is reported to have disapproved of sprinkling the water over the grave, for it is like plastering it.

Similar statements are found in all the works of the Hanafi Fiqh.

Some jurists have added that writing on the graves is also forbidden.

Al-Qadi Ibrahim al-Hanafi said: "The domes erected over the tombs must be demolished, for they are founded on the disobedience and opposition to the Prophet (peace and blessings of Allah be upon him)."

Similar views have been reported from the Shafi', Hanbali, and Maliki jurists. Why should this be not prohibited as the Messenger of Allah (peace and blessings of Allah be upon him) has forbidden it?

'A'ishah, (Allah be pleased with her) reported the Messenger of Allah (peace and blessings of Allah be upon him) as saying during his illness from which he could not recover: 'May Allah curse the Jews and Christians. They took the graves of their prophets as mosques.' She ('A'ishah) reported: Had it not been so, his (Prophet's) grave would have been in an open place, (but it could not be so), for he feared that it might not be taken as a mosque.

The Messenger of Allaah (peace and blessings of Allah be upon him prohibited plastering a grave, sitting on it, and to build upon it. Narrated by Muslim in his Saheeh (v.7 p.37)

On the authority of Jundab bin Abdullaah (Allah be pleased with him) who said: I heard the Messenger of Allaah (peace and blessings of Allah be upon him) say five days before he passed away: "Verily I free myself to Allaah that I took one of you as a close companion; indeed Allaah took me as a close companion like He took Ibraheem as a close companion. If I were to take a close companion from my Ummah I would have taken Abu Bakr as a close companion. Verily those that came before you used to take the graves of their Prophets and righteous people as places of worship. So do not take the graves as places of worship, verily I prohibit you from this." Narrated by Muslim (v.5 p.13) with an-Nawawee's checking.

On the authority of Ayesha that Umm Salamaah (Allah be pleased with them) mentioned to the Messenger (peace and blessings of Allah be upon him) about a church she saw in Ethiopia. It was said that it was called Mareeya. She mentioned to him what she saw of the pictures inside it. The Messenger Allaah (peace and blessings of Allah be upon him) said: 'They are a people, that if a righteous worshipper or a righteous man dies among them then they build a place of worship on his grave, and then they paint these pictures in it, they are the most evil of creation with Allaah.' Narrated by Bukharee (v.2 p.78)

On the authority of Abu Murthid al-Ghanawee who said that the Messenger of Allaah (peace and blessings of Allah be upon him) said: 'Do not sit on graves and do not pray towards them.' Narrated by Muslim (v.7 p.38)

This shows the consensus of the Sahabah, Tabi'is, their followers, and of all Imams, Jurists, and Muhadith of the Salaf against grave worship.

May Allah send Salah and Salam on the Prophet (peace and blessings of Allah be upon him), his household, his companions and on those who followed them.